THE
VOTE

MAKING YOUR VOICE HEARD

Linda Scher

A Blackbirch Graphics Book

RAINTREE
STECK-VAUGHN
PUBLISHERS

Austin, Texas

A Blackbirch Graphics Book

Printed in Mexico.

1 2 3 4 5 6 7 8 9 0   RRD   97 96 95 94 93 92

Library of Congress Cataloging-in-Publication Data

Scher, Linda.
      The vote: making your voice heard/ written by Linda Scher
            p.   cm.— (Good citizenship library)
      Includes bibliographical references (p.   ) and index.
      Summary: Discusses who can vote, how and where to vote, who votes and who does not, and how to vote wisely.
            ISBN 0-8114-7357-0   ISBN 0-8114-5585-8 (softcover)
            1. Elections—United States—Juvenile literature. 2. Voting—United States—Juvenile literature. [1. Voting. 2. Elections.] I. Title II. Series.
JK1978.S34 1993
324.973—dc20   92-14474
                                                                       CIP
                                                                       AC

Acknowledgments and Photo Credits

Cover: ©Dirck Halstead/Gamma-Liaison; p. 4: ©Stephanie FitzGerald; p. 6: ©Gary Payne/Gamma-Liaison; pp. 8, 10, 16, 17: AP/Wide World Photos; p. 11: The National Archives; p. 12: North Wind Picture Archives; p. 14: ©Elliott Erwitt/Magnum Photos; p. 15: Library of Congress Collection; p. 18: ©John Barr/Gamma-Liaison; p.20: AP/Wide World Photos; p. 23: ©James Pozarik/Gamma-Liaison; p. 29: ©Diana Walker/ Gamma-Liaison; p. 30: ©Eric Bouvet/Gamma-Liaison; p. 36: UPI/ Bettmann Newsphotos; p. 38: ©S. Ferry-Liais/Gamma-Liaison; p. 41: ©Michael Abramson/Gamma-Liaison; p. 43 (upper left): ©Barry Thumma/AP/Wide World Photos; p. 43 (upper right): ©Jim Bourg/ Gamma-Liaison; p. 43: (right center): ©Cynthia Johnson/Gamma-Liaison; p. 43 (lower right); ©Wilfredo Lee/AP/Wide World Photos; p. 43 (lower left): ©C. Halebian/Gamma-Liaison; p. 45: ©Richard Glassman.

Photo research by Grace How.

Contents

Who Can Vote?

Before you reach 18, the official voting age, you will have voted many times—in school elections, or as part of a social club, church group, sports team, or family. Voting is a way of making decisions—better than fighting and much less dangerous. Americans do it all the time. They raise their hands or take out pencil and paper. Voting is so much a part of our lives that Americans talk about "voting with their pocketbooks" by buying or not buying certain products, or "voting with their feet" by walking out of activities they don't like.

Right now your decision-making affects family, friends, and classmates. But in a few years your influence as a voter will extend much further. At 18

Opposite:
Voting gives citizens a voice in America's democracy.

5

you can join the millions of Americans making decisions for their city, state, and country. You may help decide whether your community wants a new road or where a garbage dump should be located. Your choices as a voter will determine who the nation's top political leader, the president, will be.

Voting Is a Foundation of Democracy

In a democracy, voting is the easiest and most direct way citizens have of taking part in government. "Politics is just people, convinced, one by one, to vote for one candidate over another," says Cynthia Samuels in her book, *It's a Free Country.* Voting is the way citizens let their government know what kind of job they think it is doing. Every four years the president and many thousands of other elected officials get a "report card" from the people. With their votes, Americans tell their leaders what they thought of their performance. And Americans get plenty of practice doing it, too. The United States has more than 500,000 elected officials. Each is chosen by the voters. In

Voting is an important way for citizens to participate in the community decisions that affect their lives.

addition, Americans vote on a great many issues, everything from where to build a sports arena to whether dogs may be permitted to walk on city streets without leashes.

Voting Today

Considering how important the job of a voter is, joining this club of decision makers is easy. And it's free. To vote you must be a citizen of the United States and at least 18 years of age. You must also live in the city and state where you plan to vote. Each state decides how long you must be a resident there. Our nation's leaders adopted this residency requirement for two reasons. The rule keeps dishonest politicians from bringing in people from other areas to vote in local elections. It also makes sure voters moving from other places have had some time to learn about candidates and issues in state and local elections before they vote.

Until 1971, Americans had to be 21 before they could vote. In that year the Constitution was amended, or changed, to make 18 the legal voting age. This change, the Twenty-sixth Amendment, was added shortly after many young American soldiers had fought in a bloody war in Vietnam. Most Americans felt that anyone old enough to fight for the United States should have the right to vote for its leaders. The states approved the Twenty-sixth Amendment very quickly—it took only three months and seven days.

How Has Voting

Changed?

For most Americans, the right to vote is not something they think much about—especially at eight or nine years old. But on March 7, 1965, eight-year-old Sheyann Webb of Selma, Alabama, was thinking a lot about this right. On that day Sheyann took the scariest walk of her life. She and 600 other people were protesting the way voting rights had been denied to African Americans in Alabama and many other states in the South. Protesters planned to march from the town of Selma to the state capital, about 54 miles away. Although Alabama Governor George C. Wallace banned the march, the protesters started out anyway. At a small bridge just outside Selma, Alabama, state troopers and local police with

Opposite: **Martin Luther King, Jr., led the civil rights movement of the 1960s. This movement changed voting laws to better include African Americans in the democratic process.**

Many protesters who marched for equal rights in the 1960s faced brutal treatment from law enforcement officials. Marchers who walked to Selma, Alabama, in 1965 were beaten and sprayed with fire hoses to stop their protests.

tear gas and clubs met the marchers. The troopers warned them to turn back. They did not. Sheyann recalled what happened next.

> As we approached the bridge, I was getting frightened more and more and as we got to the top of the bridge, I could see hundreds of policemen, state troopers . . . . and I began to just cry. . . . I saw people being beaten and I began to just try to run home as fast as I could. . . . It was like I was running for my life. . . .

As troopers and policemen beat back the marchers, cameras and tape recorders whirred and clicked. Pictures of bloodied protesters were splashed across the front pages of newspapers and shown on television screens around the world. The news coverage helped build support for new laws to ensure the rights of African American voters. Sheyann's frightening walk brought Americans a step forward in the fight for voting rights that began when our country was formed.

White Males Only

When our nation celebrated its first Fourth of July as a free and independent country in 1776, few Americans could vote. Although our nation called itself a democracy then, only certain white males, aged 21 and over, could vote. The right to vote is called "suffrage," and it was limited to men who owned property or had a large income. The list of people who could not vote was much longer than the list of those who could. Neither women nor Native Americans nor African Americans had this right. The struggle to gain the vote for all Americans lasted into the twentieth century.

States kept the property and income requirements for voter eligibility until the 1820s. The western states were the first to lift these two requirements for white male voters. Connecticut followed, and Massachusetts and New York did so a few years later. By the mid-1800s, most white males, rich or poor, could vote.

The goal to gain the vote for African-American males was advanced a step in 1870, when the Fifteenth Amendment was added to the Constitution. Congress passed and the states ratified (approved) this amendment not long after the Civil War ended.

The Constitution was written by wealthy white men who did not realize that women and African Americans would need to vote.

This amendment does not specifically mention African Americans, but makes it illegal to keep citizens from voting because of their race. For the next 20 years many blacks in the South did vote and some even held political offices. But beginning in the early 1890s, white southern leaders found new ways to deny African Americans their right to vote.

One was the "poll tax." Many southern states imposed poll taxes, or fees, that had to be paid by voters before voting. These taxes kept many poor blacks and whites from voting. States also had literacy tests that kept out those who could not read. Even those who could read faced impossible tests. In Mississippi, black voters had to answer a 22-question test. One question required them to explain one of the 286 sections of Mississippi's state

Black Americans throughout the country rejoiced when slavery was abolished by the Thirteenth Amendment.

constitution. White election officials decided if the answers were "correct." With this bias, it was not surprising that most whites passed such tests; African Americans usually failed them. In Louisiana, the number of votes cast by African Americans shrank from 130,000 in 1896 to 5,000 in 1900. As a result of these unfair requirements, African Americans lost their voting rights in the South despite the Fifteenth Amendment. Many who tried to vote received threats against their lives or lost their jobs. These practices continued into the 1960s. Fannie Lou Hamer, a leader in the fight for voting rights in Mississippi, recalled how she tried to "register," or sign up, to vote in 1962:

I traveled 26 miles to the county courthouse to try to register to become a first-class citizen. I was fired [August 31] from a plantation where I had worked . . . for 18 years. [The plantation owner told Hamer:] "Fannie Lou, you have been to the courthouse to try to register. . . . We are not ready for this in Mississippi." I said, "I didn't register for you. I tried to register for myself."

Fannie Lou Hamer and many other African Americans were tired of being treated as second-class citizens. They wanted the rights given to them by the U.S. Constitution, and were willing to fight for them. Led by the Rev. Martin Luther King, Jr., they launched a drive for equal rights in the 1960s. The march in Selma, Alabama, that Sheyann Webb

13

joined was a part of this fight. So were many other protests throughout the South. Terrible scenes of the police beating protesters and of black churches being bombed helped win public support for new laws to protect the rights of African Americans. So did protests like the August 1963 march on Washington, D.C., led by Martin Luther King. More than 200,000 people crowded the streets of the nation's capital.

Urged on by leaders like Dr. King and President Lyndon Johnson (served 1963–1969), Congress began passing laws to end this unfair treatment. The Twenty-fourth Amendment became law in 1964. It ended poll taxes in national elections. The Voting Rights Act of 1965 outlawed literacy tests and allowed federal officials to register voters if local officials refused. Once barriers to voting fell, thousands of new African American voters came to the polls and elected new leaders to represent them.

Women Get the Vote

Like African Americans, women fought hard for suffrage. Alice Paul (1885–1977) was an important leader in the fight for women's rights. In her writings, she recalled how she felt about not being able to vote:

> Well, to me it was shocking that a government of men could [so despise] a movement that was asking for nothing except such a simple little thing as the right to vote.

President Lyndon Baines Johnson did much to help African Americans gain voting equality in the 1960s.

American women first organized to fight for their voting rights in 1848. At a convention for women's rights held in Seneca Falls, New York, leaders called on men and women to work for women's suffrage. But most Americans, men and women, thought such ideas were strange. At first, the women's suffrage movement had few supporters. Many people argued against it. Some said women were not as smart as men and would not use their vote wisely. Others claimed voting should be based on ability to serve in the army. In Congress, some senators argued that giving women voting rights would take too much time away from their most important duties—caring for children and doing housework.

After the Civil War (1861–1865) the women's suffrage movement became more active and better organized. By 1870, Susan B. Anthony and Elizabeth Cady Stanton had founded the National Woman Suffrage Association to work on the federal level for the vote.

Women did have some supporters among the men in Congress. Beginning in 1878, an amendment was introduced to Congress every year calling for women's suffrage. And just as regularly, most members of Congress voted against it. By 1890, the National Woman Suffrage Association had merged with Lucy Stone's American Woman Suffrage Association to form one large organization called the National American Woman Suffrage Association

Women's rights advocate Susan B. Anthony founded the National Woman Suffrage Association with Elizabeth Cady Stanton in 1870.

Suffragists marched to the White House in 1917 to urge the government to give women the vote.

(NAWSA). By 1913, when Woodrow Wilson became president, nine states and one territory had given women the vote, but the nation was no closer to making women's suffrage the law of the land.

Then, on Wilson's inauguration day, a peaceful parade for women's suffrage through the nation's capital turned ugly. Men along the parade route spat on the women, shoved and slapped them, threw cigarette butts at them, and tore their clothes and banners. Troops from a nearby army base had to be called to keep order.

To win this "simple little thing," Alice Paul decided direct action was needed. Paul had members of her Woman's Party picket the White House. They carried signs calling for women's rights. Their protests embarrassed the president and he had them arrested. In jail, many were poorly treated. Some prisoners went on hunger strikes and had to be force-fed.

Other women, led by Carrie Chapman Catt, worked more quietly to win nationwide support. They wrote letters, filed petitions, and called on members of Congress, urging them to pass an amendment giving women the right to vote. Marches, arrests, and political action put women's suffrage in the spotlight. And yet, by 1917, when the United States entered World War I, many in Congress still opposed giving the vote to women.

During the war, women gladly stepped in to take over the factory jobs of soldiers sent overseas.

More and more Americans saw how unfair it was to expect women to support the war effort but refuse them equal voting rights. In 1918, President Wilson came to the Senate to urge its members to pass a women's suffrage amendment. He pointed out how hard women had worked:

We have made partners of the women in this war. Shall we admit them only to partnership of . . . . [work] and not a partnership of privilege? This war could not have been fought . . . by America if it had not been for the services of the women. . . .

The senators refused President Wilson's plea for an amendment in 1918. But one year later the president called a special session of Congress to try again. This time the men of Congress were ready to give women the vote. Although its members passed the Nineteenth Amendment, the fight was not yet over. Before the amendment could become law, three-fourths of the states had to "ratify," or approve, it. It took another 13 months before the thirty-sixth state (Tennessee) ratified the Nineteenth Amendment in 1920.

Alice Paul, standing second from right, organized a protest march at the 1920 Republican convention to demand ratification of the Nineteenth Amendment.

How and Where

Do You Vote?

In the 1890s, a group of very crooked New York City politicians (known as Tammany Hall) found a sure way to win elections. Here's how Tim Sullivan, one of the leaders, explained it. On Election Day, a party worker rounded up jobless men and offered them a day's wages. Then he took them to a polling place to vote. At that time most men wore beards, mustaches, and long sideburns. After voting once, Sullivan's voters went to a barbershop and had their beards shaved off. Then they moved on to a new polling place to vote again. Sullivan reminded his friends to "vote early and often." Most had voted four or five times for Sullivan's favorite candidates by the end of the day.

Opposite:
Before a person can actually vote, he or she must register in the town or city in which he or she lives.

19

A typical voting place in 1860, the year in which Abraham Lincoln was elected president.

The Registration Process

In the late 1800s, tricks like these were common in many cities. Dishonest voters could vote "early and often" because most big cities had few rules for keeping track of voters. To correct such problems, today all states have strict rules about who can vote on Election Day. For example, voters must have lived in the state for at least 30 days before the election, and in every state but North Dakota, no voters can vote on Election Day unless they have first registered. To register, a person must have his or her name officially placed on the voters' rolls in his or her home state. Usually, a voter must register at a town or city hall located near the voter's home.

All states try to make it easy for citizens to register. In many states people can register at public libraries, shopping centers, schools, and at places where a driver's license is obtained. A few states allow voters to register by mail. States differ over how long before an election voters must register. Maine, Minnesota, and Wisconsin, for example, allow voters to register on Election Day. Other states require voters to sign up at least 30 days before an election. To find out where to register, voters can call the Board of Elections of their county. Many communities also have a group called the League of Women Voters, whose job it is to help all voters.

The registration process is simple, but a little different in each state. Voters show something that proves they are who they say they are and where they live, and sign a form similar to the one at the bottom of this page. Often people use a driver's license to prove their identity and address.

Voter registration forms help local governments keep track of who is voting in their area.

TOWNSHIP	PRECINCT NO.	☐ OR ☐ IN OUT	IF IN, WHICH CITY OR TOWN	DO NOT WRITE ABOVE—FOR BOARD OF ELECTIONS USE ONLY

VOTER CERTIFICATION

I hereby certify that the information I shall give with respect to my qualifications and identity is true and correct to the best of my knowledge.

REGISTRATION OATH

I do solemnly swear (or affirm) that I will support the Constitutions of the United States and the State of North Carolina; that I will have been a resident of this State and this precinct for 30 days by the date of the next election; that I have not registered, nor will I vote in any other county or State, so help me God.

REGISTRATION DECLARATION MADE UNDER OATH BY VOTER

LAST NAME	FIRST NAME	MIDDLE/MAIDEN NAME	(PARTY) AFFILIATION

RESIDENCE: NUMBER & STREET OR ROAD NAME OR RURAL ROUTE AND BOX NO.	CITY OR TOWN	ZIP CODE	SEX MALE ☐ FEMALE ☐	RACE

PLACE OF BIRTH (County, State or Country)	DATE OF BIRTH MONTH DAY YEAR	DATE OF REGISTRATION MONTH DAY YEAR	DATE OF RESIDENCE	MISC. INFORMATION: DATE & COURT OF NATURALIZATION

I HAVE ADMINISTERED BOTH THE ABOVE VOTER CERTIFICATION AND THE ABOVE REGISTRATION OATH.

I HAVE TAKEN AND SWORN TO (OR AFFIRMED) BOTH THE ABOVE VOTER CERTIFICATION AND THE ABOVE REGISTRATION OATH.

DAYTIME TELEPHONE NO.

_____
SIGNATURE OF REGISTRATION OFFICIAL

_____
SIGNATURE OF VOTER

WAKE COUNTY VOTER REGISTRATION FORM   10184018

Registration puts every voter's name on a list of qualified voters. To make voting easier, every city or county is divided into areas called precincts, districts, or wards. Each of these areas has a special place where its local people go to vote. People can vote only at the polling place in the area where they live. On Election Day, officials at each voting place have a list of registered voters for their polling place. They check each voter's name against this list before ballots are cast. In most states voters have to register only once, unless they move to a new county. In a few states, voters must register again every few years even if they have not moved.

The Polling Place

By law, polling places must be easy to reach for all voters in a precinct. Schools, fire stations, and courthouses are some places that serve as polling places on Election Day. One place that cannot be used for voting is a bar. Voters cannot cast their ballots in a place where alcohol is served. This law dates back to the time when heavy drinkers swapped votes for whiskey. In earlier times, some citizens sold their vote to the candidate most willing to pay them with a drink.

Another law prevents a different kind of influence buying. On Election Day, supporters cannot give out pamphlets or other campaign material for their favorite candidates within a certain number of feet from the polling place.

Voting by Party

Do you know people who refer to themselves as Democrats or Republicans? America has two major political parties. Each party picks candidates to run in national and state elections. When people register to vote, they can do so as a member of one of these two parties. Or they can register as Independents. This means that they don't consider themselves members of either major party.

In most states, only voters who register as Republicans or Democrats can vote in a primary election. This is an occasion to vote to pick a party's candidate for a regular election. Political parties hold primaries to choose candidates for president, members of Congress, and other national offices. Voters in primaries can also choose candidates for state offices, such as governor. People registered as

There are many laws about how polling places must be run. Among other things, polling places may not serve alcohol and may not allow campaign workers near the polls.

Political Parties and Their Candidates in 1988

Party	Candidate	Popular Vote	Percent	Electoral Vote
Republican	George Bush (Tex.) and Dan Quayle (Ind.)	48,881,011	53.37	426
Democrat	Michael S. Dukakis (Mass.) and Lloyd Bentsen (Tex.)	41,828,350	45.67	112
Libertarian	Ron Paul (Tex.)	431,499	0.47	—
New Alliance	Leonora Fulani (N.Y.)	218,159	0.24	—
Populist	David Duke	48,267	0.05	—
Consumer	Eugene J. McCarthy	30,510	0.03	—
American Independent	James Griffin	27,818	0.03	—
National Economic Recovery	Lyndon H. LaRouche, Jr.	25,082	0.03	—
Right-to-Life	William Mara	20,497	0.02	—
Worker's League	Ed Winn	18,579	0.02	—
Socialist Workers	James Warren	13,338	0.01	—
Peace Freedom	Herbert Lewin	10,312	0.01	—
Prohibition	Earl F. Dodge	7,984	0.01	—
Worker's World	Larry Holmes	7,719	0.01	—
Socialist	Willa Kenoyer	3,800	—	—
American	Delmar Dennis	3,456	—	—
Grassroots	Jack Herer	1,949	—	—
Independent	Louie Youngkite	372	—	—
Third World Assembly	John Martin	235	—	—
Other		6,934	—	—

Total vote   91,585,871
Bush plurality*   7,052,661

*Excess of votes received to win an election.

Republicans help select Republican candidates. Voters registered as Democrats take part in primaries to choose the candidates they hope will beat the Republicans on Election Day.

From Paper Ballots to Computers

It is Election Day. The year is 2020 or maybe sooner. You walk into your living room and turn on your computer. A ballot appears on your computer screen showing the choices for president. You press a button on the computer or on a touch-tone telephone that sends your vote to the local election board over the telephone wires. Does this sound like science fiction or fantasy? Many experts think it's a realistic picture of what elections may be like in the future. Computers are already changing the way in which people vote.

In colonial times, Virginia voters called out their votes to an election official. Supporters of the candidates stood nearby, listening carefully to hear how each man voted. Rich candidates often rewarded loyal voters with food, drink, or money. Some also found ways to punish those members of the community who voted against them.

By the 1800s, voters had more privacy: they wrote their choices on paper ballots. But in most places, finding out how everyone voted was still easy. Government officials did not print official ballots. They depended on political parties to supply them. Each party offered voters a different color ballot, making it easy to tell how everyone voted. By 1888, however, Americans were making their choices in secret. They no longer worried about what anyone else would think. By then all states were using ballots printed and given out by the government. Along with official ballots, election officials also set aside private areas for marking ballots. These changes made elections more honest and ended the careers of many crooked politicians.

Today paper ballots are rare. Almost everywhere they have been replaced by voting machines. The first voting machines were mechanical. Voters pulled a large lever to close the curtains around a voting booth, and then made their choices by switching little levers next to each candidate's name. Another pull of the large lever opened the curtains and registered the votes at the same time. Such machines cut the time for vote counting from days to hours. But lever machines may soon join the horse and buggy in history museums. Although many states still use lever machines, no companies make them any more. Weighing anywhere from 700 pounds to a ton, they now seem heavy and slow compared to modern systems of computer voting that are becoming more widely used.

Today almost all new voting machines use some form of computer to operate. With some systems, voters use a special light pen to mark their ballots. With others, they punch small holes in punch cards. The punched or marked cards are fed into high-speed card-reading machines. These machines turn holes or marks into numbers a computer can count. And they do it quickly, too, at the rate of 1,000 cards per minute.

Whether voters use a computer or a lever machine, the vote-counting process is the same in every state. All votes are stored in the machine at the local precinct until the polling place closes. Once the polls are officially closed, election officials from both major political parties count the votes and report their findings to their state or county election boards. Newer electronic voting machines

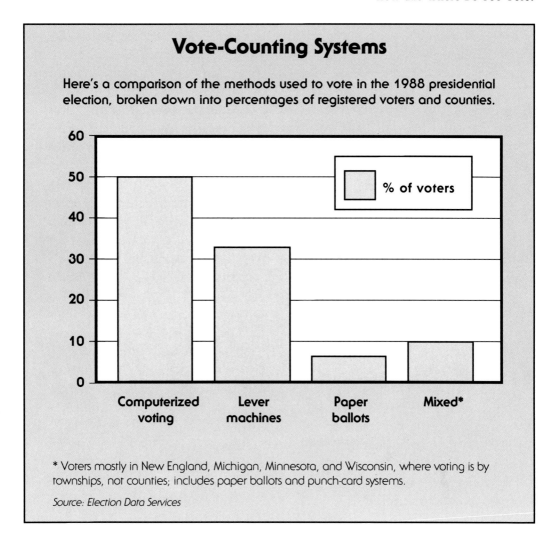

Vote-Counting Systems

Here's a comparison of the methods used to vote in the 1988 presidential election, broken down into percentages of registered voters and counties.

% of voters

Computerized voting — Lever machines — Paper ballots — Mixed*

* Voters mostly in New England, Michigan, Minnesota, and Wisconsin, where voting is by townships, not counties; includes paper ballots and punch-card systems.

Source: Election Data Services

send this information electronically from each precinct to a central reporting station within each county. The use of electronic voting machines and computer-assisted voting greatly increases the speed at which votes can be counted. In the not-too-distant future, Americans may be able to find out who the nation's president is within an hour of closing time at the polls.

Did you know that when Americans go to the polls in November to vote for president and vice-president, they are actually voting for a group of people called electors? A vote for the Democratic candidate for president is a vote for Democratic electors. A ballot cast for the Republican contender selects Republican electors. In December, at state capitals all over the United States, these electors cast the votes that officially send the nation's new leader to the White House. There are 538 electors, and together they make up the Electoral College.

The Electoral College is not a school. Most of its members never meet each other, and their jobs exist for only a few months during presidential election years. The electors for each state are chosen according to state law, and the process is a little different in each state. Typically, the state Republican and Democratic parties each choose lists of electors early in the election year. Every state chooses as many electors as it has members of Congress. For example, Indiana has 2 senators and 10 representatives, so it picks 12 electors. Since 1961, when the Twenty-third Amendment became law, the

District of Columbia has also had three electors. That brings the total number of electors to 538.

After the polls close on Election Day, the millions of votes cast by Americans are counted. This total is known as the popular vote. The popular vote is used to determine how many electoral votes each candidate will get. In each state, the candidate with the most popular votes gets all of a state's electoral votes. For example, in the 1988 election, close to 1.3 million voters in Indiana cast their ballots for Republican George Bush. Although over 860,000 voters favored Michael Dukakis, the Democratic party candidate, Bush received all 12 electoral votes from Indiana.

Because of Bush's victory in Indiana, in 1988 Indiana's Republican electors met at the state capital in December to cast the state's 12 electoral votes. On this same day, electors in other states met at their state capitals to cast electoral votes for the winning candidates. Although by this time Americans already know who their new president and vice-president will be, the electoral votes from each state go to the nation's capital to be counted before a joint

session of Congress early in January. A candidate must receive no less than 270 votes, a majority of all electoral votes, to be officially declared president. If no one candidate wins a majority, congresspeople in the House of Representatives choose the president from among the top three candidates. The Senate makes the choice for vice-president if no candidate wins over half the electoral votes in this race.

The Electoral College exists partly because our country's founders did not favor direct election of the president by the people. They lacked confidence in the ordinary voter. Instead, they favored choosing electors who would use their own best judgment in selecting national leaders. Today many people feel that the direct election of presidents by popular vote works so well that the Electoral College is no longer needed.

4

Who Votes and

Who Doesn't?

 Until 1988, Hikmat Faraj had no vot-
ing rights, although he had been living
in the United States for at least five
years. Faraj was born and grew up in
the country of Iraq. In September 1988, he became
an American citizen. Two months later, Faraj voted
for the first time in a free election. Faraj will always
remember the day, because in his native land ordinary people had no part in government. Their
leader, Saddam Hussein, made all the decisions for
the country. In Iraq, said Faraj, "They tell you
whom to vote for."

Faraj waited eagerly for his first chance to express
his opinion as an American. He was puzzled by the
way many people in his newly adopted country felt

Opposite:
**A Russian
immigrant waits
at the airport to
begin a new life
in America.**

31

about this right. "I think Americans . . . don't realize what it's like in the other parts of the world. People who immigrate value the rights of the individual, such as voting, much more."

Sadly, Faraj is right. Many Americans don't take their voting rights seriously. Compared to citizens of other democracies, Americans have a terrible voting record. Unfortunately, it keeps getting worse. In Abraham Lincoln's day, more than 80 percent of all eligible voters voted. Three fourths of all Americans were still going to the polls in 1892. But voter turnout, the number of people who vote, has been steadily shrinking for a long time. In the 1988 presidential election, only about half of all eligible voters came to the polls. In Georgia, South Carolina, and Washington, D.C., even fewer voters turned out. In these places, only 2 out of every 10 people who could have voted did so.

In election years when Americans are not choosing a new president, the bad news is even worse. Only 36 percent of the eligible voters went to the polls in 1990. Thus, only one third of all eligible voters made important political decisions for the rest of us. In 1990, about 67 million Americans came out to vote in national elections. This is fewer than the number of Americans who watch the Super Bowl on television each January.

Turnout hits bottom in local elections, such as races for mayor or city council. Unless these elections come at the same time as a race for president

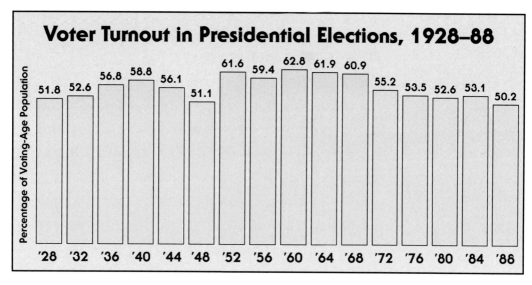

Voter Turnout in Presidential Elections, 1928–88

Percentage of Voting-Age Population

'28	'32	'36	'40	'44	'48	'52	'56	'60	'64	'68	'72	'76	'80	'84	'88
51.8	52.6	56.8	58.8	56.1	51.1	61.6	59.4	62.8	61.9	60.9	55.2	53.5	52.6	53.1	50.2

or members of Congress, fewer than 25 percent of voters turn out. Look around your classroom sometime and try to imagine letting one fourth of the students make decisions about your school, your streets, and your taxes, while the rest of the class decides not to take part.

Most democratic countries have a better record on voting than the United States. At least 8 out of every 10 voters in Belgium, Italy, Australia, and Sweden cast their votes on Election Day. When experts compared the U.S. voter with voters in 19 other countries in 1984, Americans lagged behind all but one country in the percentage of eligible voters who came to the polls. In Switzerland, the country with fewer voters than the United States, the citizens seem so pleased with life in their nation that they see little reason to vote. But polls show that most Americans are *not* that happy with their government or its leaders, but that doesn't make them get out and vote.

Voters and Nonvoters

Although there is no such thing as a typical American voter, we do know quite a bit about who votes and who doesn't. People who finish college vote more than dropouts or people with only a high school education. Rich people vote more than poor ones, whites more than nonwhites, city residents more than those in small towns. Doctors, lawyers, bankers, and other professional people go to the polls more often than farmers or factory workers.

Where you live also makes a difference in how often you vote. Southerners go to the polls less often than Americans living in other parts of the country. This may be because more poor or rural people live there. Although women fought hard for their voting rights, until recently they voted less often than men. In the 1988 election for president, however, about the same number of men and women cast votes. Will women go on to be better voters than men? Experts will study results of the 1992 election and beyond before giving an opinion.

Young Americans have the nation's worst voting record. People aged 18 to 24 vote less often than any other group. In 1988, only one in three young people voted for president. Twice as many people ages 45 to 64 went to the polls. Why are younger Americans less likely to vote? Possibly because their minds are on other things during those years. They may be busy looking for jobs, going to college, dating, or starting a family. Many are also on the go, moving from one state or city to another. This makes it harder to meet requirements for registering to vote.

The nation's best voters are midde-aged people. They take their voting rights seriously and go to the polls more often than any other group. People in their sixties and seventies vote less often than middle-aged people, but more than young voters.

Why People Don't Vote

In 1988, on Election Day, 31-year-old Ron Grey of Sacramento, California, did not vote. When a newspaper reporter asked him why, he replied, "They [politicians] are going to do the same thing whether I vote or not." Like Grey, many people don't vote because they don't think their individual votes will make a difference. Others say the reason they don't vote is that registering and getting to the polls takes too much time. Nonvoters say they are turned off by negative ads or are confused about whom to vote for. Still others feel that all the candidates are pretty much alike, or that no matter who is elected, the government does not care about or understand the needs of the people.

Presidents John F. Kennedy (served 1961–1963) and Lyndon B. Johnson both knew just how much every vote does count. Kennedy beat Richard Nixon in the presidential election of 1960 by less than two tenths of one percent of the national vote. In 1948, Democrats in his home state of Texas chose Johnson to run for senator by just 87 votes. He went on to serve in Congress and to become our nation's 36th president. Perhaps because of this, President Johnson felt strongly about the right to vote. He called it "the most basic right without which all others are meaningless. . . ."

Attracting More Voters

Some Americans are doing more than just worrying about no-show voters. They are trying to improve voter turnout. One idea they have is to make registration easier. Many states have changed their laws to allow voters to register when they get their driver's license. Some allow voters to register by mail, using a postcard that can be picked up at banks, post offices, and grocery stores. Other states may go to Election Day registration. Another idea is to move elections from a weekday to a weekend, when fewer people are at work.

Another way to make it easier for people to vote is the "absentee ballot." This allows voters to vote by mail sometime before Election Day. At one time, it was mostly people in the armed forces, college students living outside their home state, and Americans in foreign countries who voted by absentee ballot. This form

John F. Kennedy campaigned with his wife, Jacqueline, in the 1960 presidential election.

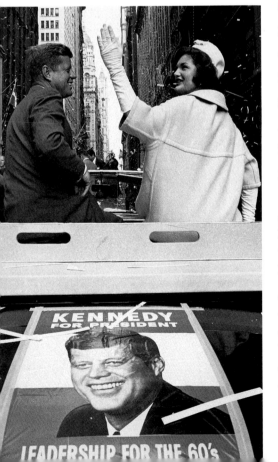

KENNEDY
FOR PRESIDENT

LEADERSHIP FOR THE 60's

Not everyone over age 18 has the right to vote. Aliens do not have voting rights. An alien is a person living in the United States who has citizenship in another country. In the United States legal aliens have many of the rights of American citizens. They can own property and run a business. They are eligible to receive many public services, and their children can attend public schools. However, aliens are not allowed to vote, serve on a jury, or hold public office. These rights are only granted to citizens. As long as a person is an alien, he or she is considered to owe allegiance, or loyalty, to a foreign country.

Two groups of American citizens do not have the right to vote. One group is people who have committed serious crimes, or felonies, such as murder, kidnapping, or robbery. These are crimes that carry long prison sentences or may be punishable by death. People convicted of felonies lose their voting rights for life. Americans who live in mental hospitals or institutions and people considered by the courts to be mentally incompetent are also not allowed to vote.

of voting is on the rise even for people who expect to be in their communities on Election Day, but find it more convenient to vote early.

The U.S. government is the only western democracy that doesn't play a part in getting out the vote. Citizens in New Zealand and Australia must pay a fine to the government for not registering. In many European countries, citizens are automatically registered to vote when they reach a certain age. In some countries, government workers go door to door before each election to get out the voters. In years to come, the U.S. government may be forced to find new ways to prevent voting from becoming a "spectator sport."

How Do You Use

Your Vote Wisely?

 Let's imagine it's almost Election Day sometime in the future. You are registered to vote and know exactly where your polling place is. But with a few more weeks until Election Day, you can't decide whom to vote for. You've asked your friends and family who their favorite candidates are. But you're wondering what else you can do to make your choices good ones.

Television and the Voter

You switch on the television. Across the screen come images of a handsome middle-aged man, his wife, and their two children. The man is lovingly petting his dog. His wife and children look on, smiling their approval. Just as you start to change the channel, a soothing voice says clearly: "Vote

Opposite:
Voters face many tough choices in each election. A responsible voter will learn as much as possible about each candidate before making a final choice.

Nelson Armstrong for president: A man you can trust." On the next channel, you see a tall woman in a business suit talking to construction workers at a building site. Although you can't hear what she says, the workers are nodding their heads to show they agree with her. Then this message flashes across the screen: "Count on Rachel Katzin to keep our economy growing. A president for today and tomorrow."

As election time draws closer, television screens fill with political ads like these. Such advertisements send messages to the viewer that the candidate is a family man, a down-to-earth businesswoman, a nature lover, or a fighter for the homeless. But do these ads really give voters information they can use to make wise choices in the voting booth? Most observers say no. Political ads are designed to catch your attention and focus it on the candidate's personality. They tell you what candidates look like, but not what their experience is or how they feel about important issues. And they give the voter little help in making wise choices. Some campaign planners defend this type of campaigning. They say most Americans lose interest in voting when issues are discussed. After the 1988 election, Edward J. Rollins, an adviser to many Republican candidates, explained: "Every time you start talking about issues, you lose some of the [undecided voters who] swing back and forth. It's unfortunate, but that's the reality of the game."

Today, many voters get their first and most lasting impression of candidates through television. Voters see the candidates on news and talk shows and in campaign ads. Michael Deaver, who was Ronald Reagan's campaign manager in 1984, explained the way his team used television to help their candidate win the race for president. "We tried to create the most entertaining . . . attractive scene to fill that [TV] box, so that the cameras from the networks would have to use it."

To win over voters, candidates today are learning how to deliver 30-second radio or television messages called "sound bytes." Because they are so short, such messages catch the viewer's attention, but give little real information about where the candidate stands on issues or what he or she would do to solve a problem.

Campaigning through television and radio ads has become more and more common in recent years. In 1974, candidates used 45 percent of their budget for media activities such as campaign ads. In 1988, only 14 years later, they spent 85 percent. The total amount of money poured into advertising has gone up, too. In 1972, politicians put $25 million into political ads in the race for president. In 1988, more than $227 million went for advertising.

Some candidates use this money for negative advertising. That means a candidate pays for ads that attack his or her opponent. Sometimes these ads suggest that the candidate has done something

Ronald Reagan used the media very successfully in both his 1980 and 1984 presidential campaigns.

wrong or should be blamed for the problems voters face. But these ads rarely give facts to back up the attack. Although the ad may be untrue, the name-calling usually works. Many voters will see only the negative ad. They don't hear the other candidate's response or get more information on their own. In addition, this kind of campaigning forces candidates to use valuable TV or radio time defending themselves against such ads when they could be talking about real issues. This kind of campaigning hurts the democratic system. Many experts blamed negative campaign tactics for the low voter turnout in the election of 1988.

Finding Answers to Important Questions

One month before Election Day, you still can't decide who will get your vote for president: Rachel Katzin or Nelson Armstrong. You know what the candidates look like, because you've seen them on television, but you don't know much about either candidate's record, achievements, or stand on issues. Here are some questions you might ask to learn more: What are this candidate's qualifications for holding office? Has the candidate had any experience doing a similar kind of job? Has the candidate served as an elected official? If so, how well did he or she do this job? What has the candidate done that shows he or she is a strong and honest leader? How has the candidate voted on issues that are important to you?

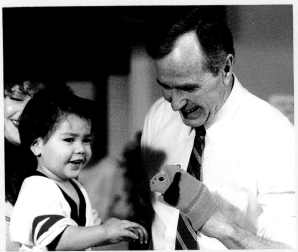

American flags and children are always among the most popular props for candidates. *Clockwise from top left:* George Bush, Paul Tsongas, Bill Clinton, Pat Buchanan, and Edmund G. Brown.

Finding the right questions to ask brings you a step closer to making wise choices as a voter. Getting the answers puts you there. During an election year, voters can find information about candidates in many places. Newspapers and magazines carry stories about candidates and issues. Close to Election Day, many newspapers also "endorse," or throw their support to, certain candidates. Newspaper editors often write editorials explaining why they think their readers should vote for the candidates they favor.

Suppose you want to learn more about how candidates Armstrong and Katzin feel about spending tax money to clean up the environment. If either has held other elected offices, you could look at the way they voted on this issue in the past. The Sierra Club and other conservation groups keep track of how national, state, and some local officials vote on environmental issues. Other groups record how politicians have voted on everything from health care to gun control.

At election time, leaflets, flyers, and letters pile up in voters' mailboxes. This flood of paper comes from the headquarters of many different candidates. Campaign literature is another way to learn about a candidate's past experiences and stands on different issues. Some literature may even provide a candidate's past voting record. Most candidates have a local or a state office you can contact to find out how they stand on the issues you care most about.

You have probably noticed that you can learn a lot about people by meeting them face to face. In local elections, candidates try to win votes by talking to community or church groups or at neighborhood get-togethers. Voters can learn by noticing how speakers answer questions. This is one reason the League of Women Voters and other groups concerned about voting hold candidate debates at election time. These debates give candidates a chance to express their opinions on issues that worry Americans, like air pollution, crime, or a sagging economy. Television brings debates between candidates for president into the home of every voter. This source of information is as close as the TV remote control.

With their votes Americans pick leaders to fill the nation's top jobs. Many Americans spend weeks or months picking out the perfect car for their family or just the right table for their kitchen. A smart shopper looks past the ads and studies the product carefully. Just as our choices as shoppers decide the quality of the goods we buy, our decisions as voters determine the quality of our nation's government and its leaders. American democracy depends on the wise choices of its voters.

The Capitol building in Washington, D.C. houses our nation's lawmakers.

45

Glossary

absentee ballot   A way to vote by mail if unable to be at the polls.

alien   A foreign-born resident who is not a naturalized citizen.

amendment   A revision or change proposed or made in a law or bill.

ballot   A paper on which a vote is cast; a secret vote.

campaign   A series of planned events by candidates for public office.

candidate   One who seeks election to office.

civil rights   The rights guaranteed to all citizens to vote and to equal treatment under the law.

democracy   Government by the people through representatives.

electoral vote   A formal vote cast by a member of the Electoral College, to elect the president and vice-president of the U.S.

issues   Matters of dispute that can be voted on.

petition   A formal, written, and signed request for specific action.

poll   A place where votes are cast.

poll tax   A fee once imposed on voters in order to vote.

precinct   A division of a voting district.

primary   A preliminary election of candidates for the general election.

protest   To speak out strongly against something.

register   To formally enter one's name on a list to vote.

suffrage   The right to vote.

ward   A division of a city or town for voting purposes.

For Further Reading

Clinton, S. *Susan B. Anthony*. Chicago: Childrens Press, 1986.

Huggins, Nathan I., ed. *Thurgood Marshall*. Broomall, Pennsylvania: Chelsea House, 1990.

McKissack, Patricia and Frederick. *The Civil Rights Movement in America from 1865 to the Present*. Chicago: Childrens Press, 1987.

Schlesinger, Arthur M. Jr., ed. *History of American Presidential Elections*. Broomall, Pennsylvania: Chelsea House, 1990.

Smith, Betsy C. *Women Win the Vote*. Westwood, New Jersey: Silver Burdett Press, 1989.

Index

Index